Plink, plonk! A white-footed kitten walks on the piano keys.

The PETS You Love

by Jennifer C. Urquhart

BOOKS FOR YOUNG EXPLORERS
NATIONAL GEOGRAPHIC SOCIETY

Safe in their yard, Conner and his dog peek over the fence. What do you think they see on the other side? Dogs make good pets and good friends.

What pet you should have depends partly on where you live. Jason and his dog, Ginger, live in the city. They look both ways before crossing a street. Jason holds the leash tightly so the dog will not run in front of a car.

In the country, Alexi has more open space to walk her dogs. Big dogs need a lot of exercise. Imagine taking care of two dogs at once!

An indoor cat like Skeezix needs
its own place to scratch or
it might tear the furniture.
Scratching its post helps the cat
keep its claws clean and sharp.

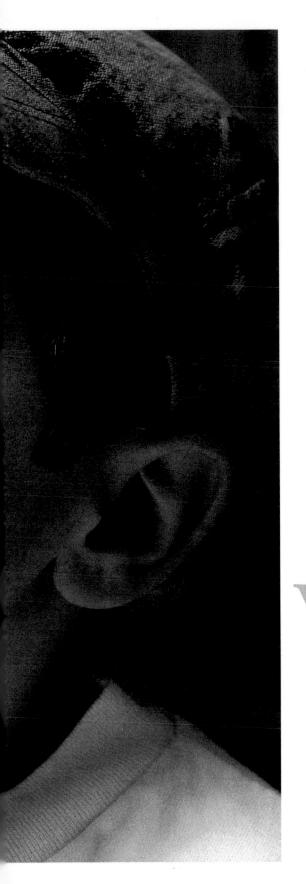

What is Dylan doing? Maybe he is teaching his bird, Kiwi, to sit on his finger. Small pets need to play outside their cages sometimes. Herbie, the gerbil, climbs out of Danny's pocket. Danny may hide a sunflower seed there for him to find. Oooh! Those little feet tickle!

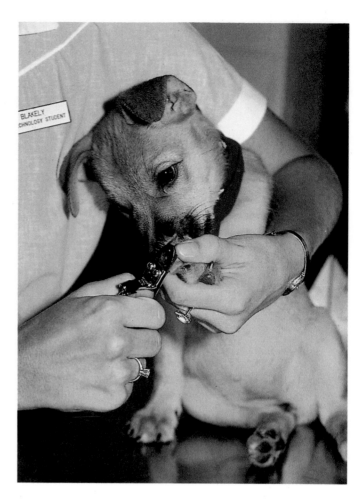

Jessie goes to the doctor. The animal doctor, called a veterinarian, is listening to the puppy's heart. Pets should have regular check-ups and shots to help keep them well.

A puppy named Casey has his nails cut with a special tool so that it does not hurt. Smokey, the tabby cat, gets his shots. His owner holds him and talks to him gently to make him feel safe. Do you think Smokey looks afraid?

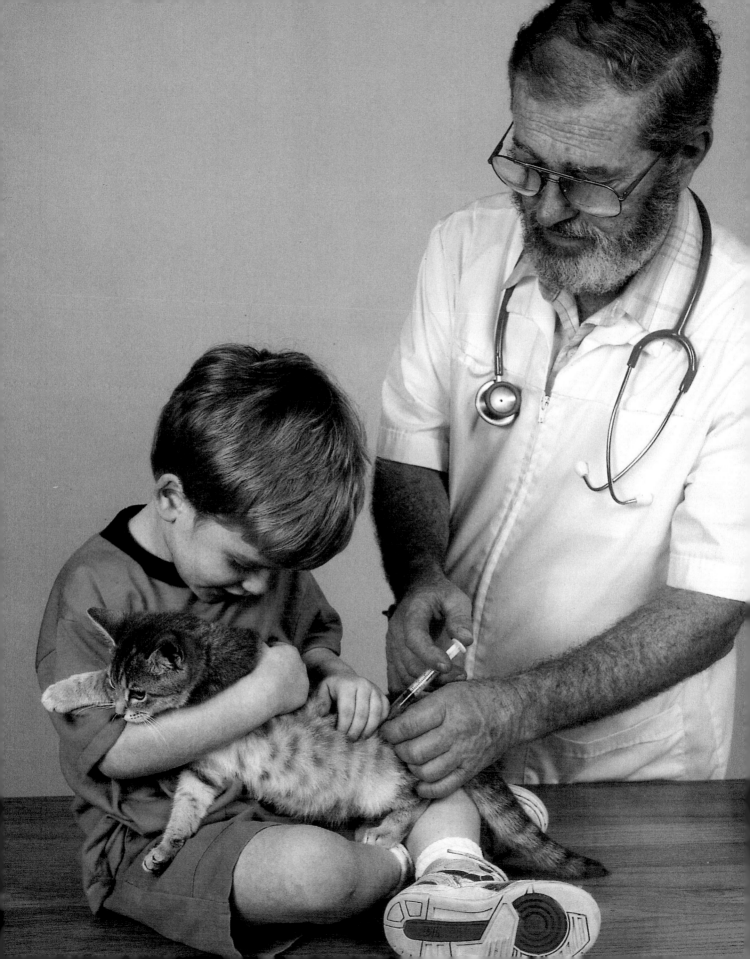

Let's play tag! Jeremy and his dog chase each other. Besides being fun, running and playing are good exercise for dogs. You have to be careful to run in a safe place, away from the road or in a fenced yard.

ogs need to be trained to stay away from danger and to behave. Sparky has lost his ball. If he fell into the pool, he might drown if he could not climb out. At the beach, Brian teaches his dog to jump high for a stick.

"What a good dog!" When house-training his puppy, a boy praises him when he uses papers as a toilet, instead of the floor.

Your pet needs your care all the time. A boy brushes his dog's long hair carefully so that it will not hurt. Brushing helps keep fleas away and also makes the dog look nice.

Teryn feeds her dog every day. This dog does not mind her patting him while he eats, but other dogs might growl. Lance is brushing his dog's teeth. Keeping the teeth clean will help the dog stay healthy.

B ath time is playtime on a hot day!
The boys scrub their dog with soap,
then rinse it all off. Next, it's their turn!
In chilly weather, you need to dry
your dog after its bath and keep it warm.

A little girl dangles a piece of yarn for her kitten to grab. If the kitten bites or scratches, the girl will gently calm it down. She does not let the kitten play with the yarn alone because it might get tangled up and choke.

Lap, lap! A young cat drinks water from a faucet. Cats need fresh water to drink every day. They like running water, just as you like a water fountain.

Cats are very clean. A mother cat licks her baby to give it a bath. This makes it feel safe and happy. When the kitten is older, it will lick itself. Cats do not usually need our help in bathing, but it is good to brush their fur regularly.

This young kitten has become scared while exploring in a tree. Its owner makes sure it is safe. Kittens can be hurt if they fall. Sometimes cats climb too high and need help getting down.

Another cat sleeps quietly in a basket. Cats like to sleep a lot. They need a safe, protected place to rest, where nothing bothers them.

The wheel spins round and round
when Greg and Mickie run.
The two golden hamsters enjoy
running and playing with toys.

Stanley kisses his rabbit, Arthur.
He holds Arthur carefully so that
he will not fall off the table.
Small pets like to be petted.
A guinea pig looks warm and cozy
as its owner dries it after a bath.

Goldfish swim around in their tank. Fish are fun to watch, and they make nice pets. They do not need much more than a clean tank, a little food, and a few plants to nibble on. This boy is scooping up his goldfish with a net. He is probably going to move them to a big, open tank, or aquarium, where they will have more room to swim and grow.

Pretty bird! The budgie likes to look in the mirror. Maybe it thinks it has a friend for company. Budgies can copy what you say if you teach them when they are young.

A girl fills a water bottle for her pet finches. She feeds them every day and makes sure their cage is clean. Birds need to eat fruits and vegetables as well as seeds. A green parrot takes a bite of celery.

Pets may love pets, too!
If different kinds of
animals get to know
each other when they are
young, they can be
friends. A guinea pig
nuzzles a cat. They
seem to like each other.
Do you think the kitty
is purring?

MORE ABOUT The PETS You Love

	DOGS	CATS	BIRDS	FISH
HOUSING	Bed and kennel needed if outdoors. Bed needed if indoors.	Simple bed needed in a quiet place indoors.	Cage and perches. An aviary—a large area covered with wire mesh—for birds kept outside in warm areas.	Aquarium is preferred. Large bowl is possible. Outdoor pool may be used for goldfish.
FOOD* (Give fresh water at all times.)	Buy bagged or canned food. Feed once or twice a day.	Buy canned and boxed cat food. Feed twice a day.	Buy birdseed at pet store. Feed once a day—enough to last all day.	Buy fish food at supermarket or pet store. Feed once or twice a day.
GENERAL CARE AND GROOMING	More than an hour a day. Brush long coats daily, short coats weekly. Bathe every 3 months, or as needed.	More than 1/2 hour a day. Brush long-haired cats daily. Brush short-haired cats twice a week.	About 20 minutes a day; much longer for birds you want to tame or teach to talk.	At least an hour a week. No grooming. Clean tank weekly.
ATTENTION NEEDED	High. Spend several hours a day with your dog. Dogs enjoy companionship and play—indoors and out.	Medium. The more you play with a cat, the more affectionate it will be. Two cats keep each other company.	Medium. Birds seem happiest with some company. Having two helps keep them from becoming lonely.	Low. For the sake of the fish, it's best to have at least two for companionship.
LIFE SPAN	At least 10 years for most.	At least 10 years for most.	5 to 60 or more years, depending on breed of bird. Parakeets: 6. Parrots: 60 or more. Canaries: 5-10 years.	2-10 years.
VET CARE	Twice a year after puppy visits, plus visits for neutering or spaying, worming, or when ill.	About two visits for a kitten. Then once a year, plus visits for neutering or spaying, worming, or when ill.	When ill, or to trim beak and nails if necessary.	Only when ill.
HAZARDS TO PET	Some bones may splinter. Chocolate can cause seizures. Electrical cords are dangerous if chewed.	Some house plants are toxic. Christmas tree lights and decorations may entangle. Aspirin is toxic.	Fumes from tobacco smoke, paint, and gas. A Teflon pan heating up emits fumes deadly to small birds.	Overcrowding tank. Tapping on glass and vibrations from loud music. Overfeeding pollutes water.

*For adult animals only. The young may have different requirements.

32

Are you having trouble deciding what kind of pet to choose? There are many things to consider. This chart may help you decide. Different animals are pictured across the top, with categories of information listed on the left. If you need more details or want to learn about pets not shown here, visit a library and consult books such as those listed below.

GERBILS	HAMSTERS	RABBITS	GUINEA PIGS
Cage. Use dry aquarium or cage with wire-mesh walls (not a bird cage).	Cage. Use dry aquarium or cage with wire-mesh walls (not a bird cage).	Indoor cage or weatherproof outdoor cage needed.	Cage. Use dry aquarium or cage with wire-mesh walls (not a bird cage).
Buy pellets at pet or feed store. Feed enough so that food is always available.	Buy pellets at pet or feed store. Feed enough so that food is always available.	Buy pellets at pet or feed store. Add hay and grass cuttings. Feed once a day.	Buy pellets at pet or feed store. Add hay and source of vitamin C. Feed once a day.
About 1/2 hour a day. Clean cage once a week. No grooming.	About 1/2 hour a day. Clean cage once a week. No grooming.	1/2 hour a day. Clean cage daily. Groom short-haired weekly; long-haired, daily.	About 1/2 hour a day. Clean cage every other day. Brush long-haired often.
Medium. Easily tamed, friendly. Handle daily. Two keep each other company.	Low. Best to keep in cage alone. Handle often to keep tame.	High. Hold and pet often. Females make good companions for each other.	Medium. As friendly as gerbils; not as playful. Two will be companions.
1-5 years.	1-4 years.	5-10 years.	4-5 years.
Only when ill.	Only when ill.	Only when ill.	Only when ill.
Rough handling.	Smell of cedar shavings in bedding may be irritating.	Support hind legs when handling to prevent back injury.	Smell of cedar shavings in bedding may be irritating.

Once you have chosen your pet, you have made a real commitment. Pets have much to offer their owners, but they usually require daily care. When you go on vacation, you will have to arrange for care of your pet. It will need you all of its life. Whatever its life span, a pet can become like a member of the family; it can be very upsetting for adults as well as for children when a pet dies.

People tend to overlook some hazards to pets. It is dangerous to leave your pet in a car. Even on a cool day, the temperature inside a vehicle parked in the sun can rise rapidly to more than 100°F, and your pet may die. More nuisance than hazard are the fleas that cats and dogs may bring home. One trick is to vacuum the infested areas of the house often.

It is recommended that you have your cat or dog neutered at the appropriate age. There are many more animals than homes for them.

ADDITIONAL READING

Cats: All About Them, by Alvin and Virginia Silverstein. (New York: Lothrop, Lee & Shephard Co., 1978.) Family reference.
The Complete Book of the Dog, edited by David W. MacDonald. (New York: Holt, Rinehart and Winston, 1985.) Family reference.
A Practical Guide to Impractical Pets, by Emil P. Dolensek, D.V.M., and Barbara Burn. (New York, Viking Press, 1976.) Family reference.

Cover: A new friend! Joshua plays gently with his little kitten. He holds it carefully from underneath.

Lindsey gives her golden retriever, Twister, a big hug. You and your pet can make each other very happy.

Published by
The National Geographic Society, Washington, D. C.
Gilbert M. Grosvenor, *President and Chairman of the Board*
Michela A. English, *Senior Vice President*
Robert L. Breeden, *Executive Adviser to the President for Publications and Educational Media*

Prepared by
The Book Division
William R. Gray, *Director*
Margery G. Dunn, *Senior Editor*

Staff for this book
Jane H. Buxton, *Managing Editor*
Greta Arnold, *Illustrations Editor*
Cinda Rose, *Art Director*
Rebecca Lescaze, *Researcher*
Karen Dufort Sligh, *Illustrations Assistant*
Karen F. Edwards, Sandra F. Lotterman, Teresita Cóquia Sison, Marilyn J. Williams, *Staff Assistants*

Engraving, Printing, and Product Manufacture
George V. White, *Director,* and Vincent P. Ryan, *Manager, Manufacturing and Quality Management*
Heather Guwang, *Production Project Manager*
Lewis R. Bassford, Richard S. Wain, *Production*

Consultants
Guy R. Hodge, The Humane Society of the United States, *Scientific Consultant*
Lynda Bush, *Reading Consultant*

Illustrations Credits
Ron Watts/WEST LIGHT (cover); Phoebe Dunn (1, 2-3, 22-23); Jim Erickson (4); David Brownell/THE IMAGE BANK (4-5); Donna K. Grosvenor (5); J. DiMaggio & J. Kalish/THE STOCK MARKET (6-7); Norvia Behling (7, 8 le., 8 rt., 9, 15 up.); J. Taposchaner/FPG INTL (10-11); Jean Wentworth (12-13); Roy Morsch/THE STOCK MARKET (13 up., 21, 23); Sisse Brimberg (13 lo., 29 up.); Robert Pearcy (14); Joseph H. Bailey, National Geographic Photographer (15 lo., 24 up., 25); Lew Long/THE STOCK MARKET (16-17 all); Ed Bock/THE STOCK MARKET (18-19); Joan Baron/THE STOCK MARKET (20-21); David de Lossy/THE IMAGE BANK (24 lo.); John M. Roberts/THE STOCK MARKET (26); Cosimo Scianna/THE IMAGE BANK (27); Lothar Reupert/THE IMAGE BANK (28); Paul E. Clark/NEW ENGLAND STOCK PHOTO (29 lo.); M. Schneider/ALLSTOCK (30-31); Walter Hodges/WEST LIGHT (34).

Library of Congress CIP Data
Urquhart, Jennifer C.
    The Pets You Love / by Jennifer C. Urquhart.
        p.   cm. — (Books for young explorers)
    Includes bibliographical references.
    Summary: Through pictures of and text about birds, dogs, rabbits, goldfish, and other animals with their owners, the reader can see the responsibilities and pleasures of having a pet.
    ISBN 0–87044–845–5 (regular edition) — ISBN 0–87044–850–1 (library edition)
    1. Pets—Juvenile literature. [1. Pets.] I. Title. II. Series.
SF416.2.U77   1991
636.088'7—dc20   91-19106
                                                                CIP
                                                                AC